PRESENTED TO:

_____

FROM:

_____

DATE:

_____

7

ENNEAGRAM TYPE

BETH McCORD
Your **Enneagram** Coach

THOMAS NELSON
Since 1798

Graphic Designer: Jane Butler, Well Refined Creative Director, wellrefined.co
Interior Designer: Emily Ghattas
Cover Designer: Greg Jackson at Thinkpen Design

ISBN-13: 978-1-4002-1575-1

Printed in China

19 20 21 22 23 GRI 10 9 8 7 6 5 4 3 2 1

Contents

CONTENTS

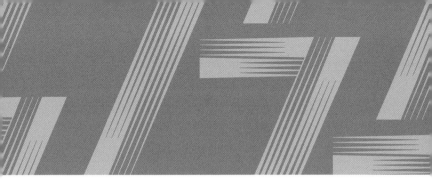

Foreword

I was looking through a children's picture book about the Enneagram. Several pages taught children (*ahem*, and me) about each type, and when I turned to the page about Type 7s, the first sentence I read simply said, "Sevens can always think of jobs they would like to have."

And I started to cry.

Reading a children's book.

Because I had lived my whole life thinking that I was discontent. That I couldn't settle on my dreams or a career and that it was a sign of weakness and immaturity, and suddenly, this one page is telling me the truth: it's okay that I can always think of other jobs.

I know that sounds bizarre, but I needed permission to dream. I had felt it in me for my whole life but didn't know it was good and right and the way God made me.

But it is. And it was learning about being an Enneagram Type 7 that started me on that path toward freedom to be me—to recognize God teaching me about myself so that I can turn around and fall more in love with Jesus and the life He has given me.

The last few years have been an intentional and sometimes painful journey to a healthier emotional, physical, and spiritual life, and the Enneagram has been one of the main tools that has been walking me toward health. Learning my motivations— recognizing unhealthy behaviors I have done for *my whole life* but understanding the why behind them, what to do when I feel pulled toward them, and how to communicate my questions and pain more clearly.

Being a Type 7 is as fun as you think it is. I absolutely love throwing parties where people make friends—whether that's in my home or on my podcast or in the comments on my Instagram posts. I love the light I get to bring into a room just by showing up. It's nothing I've done; it's just the way God made me. It's my 7-ness; it's always with me. I love to laugh loudly and wear my heart on my sleeve and invite people in to whatever I love.

The more I learn, the more I love and the more I heal. That's one of the gifts of the Enneagram. It is a tool that ensures that the more you know, the more you can become the person you really want to be. And for a Type 7 who is inclined to run from pain and be deathly afraid of being confined or trapped in a situation, I'm becoming the person who can stay, sit in it, and enjoy the beauty of perseverance and commitment. It's who I've always wanted to be anyways. And the work of the gospel in my life, the way Jesus redeems and restores and saves, is what has changed me forever.

For us Type 7s, we need books like this. We need to read every page, even the ones that hurt. We need to slow our pace and our breath and not be afraid of what we could see when the page turns. We need to face the good and the bad and let them both heal us. Let the gospel of Jesus Christ shine light on the places where fear has kept things in the dark.

For anyone who loves a Type 7, please read this book and believe it. We are as fun as you think we are, but we are also hurting. Scared. Lonely. What our faces say is not always the full story. Walk with the 7s you love, encourage them to carry joy and pain at the same time, and have fun. Always have fun.

Annie F. Downs, Bestselling Author of *100 Days to Brave*, Host of *That Sounds Fun* Podcast

Introduction

I'm so glad you're here! As an Enneagram teacher and coach, I have seen so many lives changed by the Enneagram. This is a perfect place for you to start your own journey of growth. I'll explain how this interactive book works, but first I'd like to share a little of my story.

Before I learned about the Enneagram, I often unknowingly committed *assumicide*, which is my word for damaging a relationship by assuming I know someone's thoughts, feelings, and motivations. I incorrectly guess why someone is behaving a particular way and respond (sometimes with disastrous results) without asking clarifying questions to confirm my assumptions or to find out what actually is going on. I've made many wrong and hurtful assumptions about people I dearly love, as well as destructive presumptions about myself.

When my husband, Jeff, and I were in the early years of our marriage, it was a difficult season in our relationship. For the life of me, I couldn't figure out Jeff, or myself. I had been a Christian since I was young and desired to live like Christ, but I kept running into the same stumbling blocks over and over again. I was constantly frustrated, and I longed to understand my heart's motives—*Why do I do what I do?* I figured understanding that might help jolt me out of my rut, but I didn't know where to start.

Then I learned about the insightful tool of the Enneagram, and it was exactly what I needed.

This personality typology (*ennea* for nine; *gram* for diagram) goes beyond what we do (our behaviors) and gets at *why* we do what we do (our heart's motives). And though there are just nine basic personality Types, each Type has multiple layers, allowing for numerous variations of any given personality Type.

The purpose of the Enneagram is to awaken self-awareness and provide hope for growth. Once we learn why each Type thinks, feels, and acts in specific ways, we can look at ourselves with new understanding. Then we can depend on God in new ways to reshape us. The Enneagram makes us aware of when our heart's motives are good and we are on the best path for our personality Type and when our heart is struggling and veering off course. **The Enneagram is an insightful tool, but God's truth is what sets us free and brings transformation.**

When I first learned about the Enneagram, I resonated with the Type 9—and had a good laugh when I discovered that 9s know themselves the least! But I finally had wisdom that cleared away the fog and illuminated my inner world. I kept thinking, *Oh, that's why I do that!* Everything started making sense, which brought my restless heart relief.

The Enneagram also helped me see when my heart was aligned with God's truth, misaligned to some degree, or out of alignment entirely with the person God created me to be. It would highlight where I was misunderstanding myself or those I love, and then I could use that awareness to seek transformation. Using the Enneagram from this perspective was a significant turning point for me in all my relationships, especially my marriage. My new perspective allowed me to have more compassion, kindness, forgiveness, mercy, and grace toward others and myself.

Exploring my heart has been some of the hardest—and most rewarding—work I've ever done. The process of looking at our hearts exposes who we are at the core, which highlights our need for redemption and care from God, who is always supplying us with what we need. We simply need to come to Him and depend on Him to change us from the inside out. He will give us a new internal peace, joy, and security that will help us to flourish in new and life-giving ways.

The Enneagram can function as an internal GPS, helping you understand why you and others think, feel, and behave in particular ways.

This internal GPS assists you in knowing your current location (your Main Enneagram Type) and your Type's healthiest destination (how your Type can live in alignment with the gospel).

The Enneagram also acts like a rumble strip on the highway—that boundary that makes an irritating sound when your car touches it, warning you when you're about to go off course. It keeps you from swerving into dangerous situations.

While everyone has character traits of all nine Types to varying degrees, we call only one our Main Type. In this book you will unlock some of the mysteries behind *why* you do what you do and discern ways you can grow into your best self.

If you're not sure of your Type number, that's okay! Going through the exercises will help you figure out what your Type number is. Sometimes it's helpful to find out what we're *not* as much as what we are. It's all about self-discovery and self-awareness.

If you find you resonate more with another number, that insight is valuable.

• • •

In the twenty-one entries that follow, we'll begin with a summary of your Type. Then we'll discuss topics that are general to the Enneagram and specific to your Type. Each reading will end with reflection questions—prompts to help you write out your thoughts, feelings, and gut reactions to what you have read. Putting pen to paper will help you focus and process what is going on inside you.

Before you begin, I want you to commit to observing your inner world from a nonjudgmental stance. Since God has fully forgiven us, we can observe ourselves without condemnation, guilt, or shame. Instead, we can rest in the fact that we are unconditionally loved, forgiven, and accepted based on what Christ did for us. Follow the prompts and write about your own story. Allow God to transform you from the inside out by helping you see yourself through the lens of the beautiful and amazing Type He designed you to be.

It's my privilege to walk with you as you discover who you are by examining your heart. I'm excited to be on this journey with you!

DEAR
TYPE 7
I'M THANKFUL FOR YOU BECAUSE...

You are very creative, envisioning how several areas of interest can come together to have a maximum positive impact for others. You radiate joy and enthusiasm, which allows you to see the many exciting possibilities life has to offer. Your perspective encourages others to have hope and joy in their own lives.

OVERVIEW OF THE NINE ENNEAGRAM TYPES

The Enneagram (*ennea* = nine, *gram* = diagram) is a map for personal growth that identifies the nine basic ways of relating to and perceiving the world. It accurately describes *why* you think, feel, and behave in particular ways based upon your Core Motivations. Understanding the Enneagram will give you more self-awareness, forgiveness, and compassion for yourself and others.

To find your main Type, take our FREE assessment at test.YourEnneagramCoach.com, and find the Type on the next page that has your Core Motivations—what activates and drives your thoughts, feelings, and behaviors.

Core Motivations of Each Type

Core Desires: what you're always striving for, believing it will completely fulfill you

Core Fears: what you're always avoiding and trying to prevent from happening

Core Weakness: the issue you're always wrestling with, which will remain a struggle until you're in heaven and is a reminder you need God's help on a daily basis

Core Longing: the message your heart is always longing to hear

Type 1: MORAL PERFECTIONIST

Core Desire: Having integrity; being good, balanced, accurate, virtuous, and right.

Core Fear: Being wrong, bad, evil, inappropriate, unredeemable, or corruptible.

Core Weakness: *Resentment*: Repressing anger that leads to continual frustration and dissatisfaction with yourself, others, and the world for not being perfect.

Core Longing: You are good.

Type 2: SUPPORTIVE ADVISOR

Core Desire: Being appreciated, loved, and wanted.

Core Fear: Being rejected and unwanted; being thought worthless, needy, inconsequential, dispensable, or unworthy of love.

Core Weakness: *Pride*: Denying your own needs and emotions while using your strong intuition to discover and focus on the emotions and needs of others; confidently inserting your helpful support in hopes that others will say how grateful they are for your thoughtful care.

Core Longing: You are wanted and loved.

Type 3: SUCCESSFUL ACHIEVER

Core Desire: Having high status and respect; being admired, successful, and valuable.

Core Fear: Being exposed as or thought incompetent, inefficient, or worthless; failing to be or appear successful.

Core Weakness: *Deceit*: Deceiving yourself into believing that you are only the image you present to others; embellishing the truth by putting on a polished persona for everyone (including yourself) to see and admire.

Core Longing: You are loved for simply being you.

Type 4: ROMANTIC INDIVIDUALIST

☀ **Core Desire:** Being unique, special, and authentic.

❗ **Core Fear:** Being inadequate, emotionally cut off, plain, mundane, defective, flawed, or insignificant.

⟲ **Core Weakness:** *Envy*: Feeling that you're tragically flawed, that something foundational is missing inside you, and that others possess qualities you lack.

🔥 **Core Longing:** You are seen and loved for exactly who you are—special and unique.

Type 5: INVESTIGATIVE THINKER

☀ **Core Desire:** Being capable and competent.

❗ **Core Fear:** Being annihilated, invaded, or not existing; being thought incapable or ignorant; having obligations placed upon you, or your energy being completely depleted.

⟲ **Core Weakness:** *Avarice*: Feeling that you lack inner resources and that too much interaction with others will lead to catastrophic depletion; withholding yourself from contact with the world; holding on to your resources and minimizing your needs.

🔥 **Core Longing:** Your needs are not a problem.

Type 6: LOYAL GUARDIAN

☀ **Core Desire:** Having security, guidance, and support.

❗ **Core Fear:** Fearing fear itself; being without support, security, or guidance; being blamed, targeted, alone, or physically abandoned.

❅ **Core Weakness:** *Anxiety*: Scanning the horizon of life and trying to predict and prevent negative outcomes (especially worst-case scenarios); remaining in a constant state of apprehension and worry.

🔥 **Core Longing:** You are safe and secure.

Type 7: ENTERTAINING OPTIMIST

☀ **Core Desire:** Being happy, fully satisfied, and content.

❗ **Core Fear:** Being deprived, trapped in emotional pain, limited, or bored; missing out on something fun.

❅ **Core Weakness:** *Gluttony*: Feeling a great emptiness inside and having an insatiable desire to "fill yourself up" with experiences and stimulation in hopes of feeling completely satisfied and content.

🔥 **Core Longing:** You will be taken care of.

Type 8: PROTECTIVE CHALLENGER

☀ **Core Desire:** Protecting yourself and those in your inner circle.

❗ **Core Fear:** Being weak, powerless, harmed, controlled, vulnerable, manipulated, and left at the mercy of injustice.

🗯 **Core Weakness:** *Lust/Excess*: Constantly desiring intensity, control, and power; willfully pushing yourself on others in order to get what you desire.

🔥 **Core Longing:** You will not be betrayed.

Type 9: PEACEFUL MEDIATOR

☀ **Core Desire:** Having inner stability and peace of mind.

❗ **Core Fear:** Being in conflict, tension, or discord; feeling shut out and overlooked; losing connection and relationship with others.

🗯 **Core Weakness:** *Sloth*: Remaining in an unrealistic and idealistic world in order to keep the peace, remain easygoing, and not be disturbed by your anger; falling asleep to your passions, abilities, desires, needs, and worth by merging with others to keep peace and harmony.

🔥 **Core Longing:** Your presence matters.

TYPE 7
KEY MOTIVATIONS

Sevens are motivated to experience life to the full. They want to avoid all pain and be fully satisfied and content. They want to have many possible options to choose from and escape any internal anxiety or boredom.

Overview of Type 7

The Entertaining Optimist

**Playful | Excitable | Versatile
Scattered | Escapist**

You are a joyful, enthusiastic, and social person who radiates optimism wherever you go. Lover of variety, you live life big and are eager to enjoy all the exciting experiences this world has to offer, seeing innovation and endless possibilities everywhere.

While you bring a positive outlook and happiness wherever you go, internally you are always longing for more and fearful of missing out. To you, your life experiences are often like cotton candy: they're super sweet to the taste but disappear quickly. You're constantly unsatisfied, wanting more.

You attempt to avoid pain at all costs. As soon as a situation gets complicated, painful, sad, or boring, you quickly escape to things that please you, allowing you to avoid the difficult feelings you fear. What you lack as you pursue adventure and stimulating experiences is the ability to enjoy the present and be satisfied with what you already have. You may be extremely busy, packing your schedule full and seeking fun and stimulation. Putting painful things out of your awareness, or reframing suffering into something positive without truly dealing with it will always show up in counterproductive ways throughout your life.

You can struggle in relationships, becoming scattered, uncommitted, and unreliable. People close to you may feel frustrated if you value new experiences and things more than them, or if you are unwilling to have relational depth, which often requires dealing with challenging emotions and pain together.

However, when your heart aligns with God's truth, you become more grounded in the present moment and able to savor it with a grateful heart. As you trust that God will fulfill your longings, more receptive and thoughtful qualities emerge in you. These characteristics, combined with your natural creativity and energy, make you an inspiration to others as you walk through the joy and pains of life.

Faith and the Enneagram

Is your heart a mystery to you? Do you need help using the knowledge the Enneagram offers to improve your life? If that's where you are, I'm happy to tell you that there is help and there is hope.

The Bible teaches that God cares about our heart's motives. He "sees not as man sees: man looks on the outward appearance, but the LORD looks on the heart" (1 Samuel 16:7). So we shouldn't look only at our external behaviors; we also need to examine our inner world. For most of us, it's no surprise that the heart of our problem is the problem of our heart!

Before we begin discussing the Enneagram in depth, I'd like to share my beliefs with you for two reasons: First, it's a critical part of how I'll guide you through the Enneagram principles. Second, my faith is what sustains and encourages me, and I believe the same will be true for you.

I believe the Bible is God's truth and the ultimate authority for our lives. Through it, we learn about God's character, love, and wisdom. It brings us close to Him and guides us in the best way to live. My relationship with God brought me healing and purpose before I ever heard of the Enneagram.

Jesus has not been optional for my personal growth; He has been absolutely and utterly vital. He has always come alongside me with love, compassion, and mercy.

I've always wanted my faith to be the most important part of my life, but I spent years frustrated, running into the same issues in my heart over and over again. The Enneagram helped me understand my heart's motives.

As you think about your Type, I'll help you look

at your heart, your life, and your relationships through the lens of the Enneagram. I'll also teach you ways to understand yourself and others and to develop patience and empathy for your differences.

With God working in you and helpful insights from the Enneagram to change awareness and actions, you'll grow into the person you'd like to be more than you've ever dared to dream possible.

When you place your faith in Jesus Christ as your Savior, three life-changing questions are answered, bringing you ultimate grace and freedom:

Am I fully accepted by God (even with all the mess and sin in my life)?

Yes! You are declared righteous. Christ not only purchased forgiveness for your sin but also gave you His perfect righteousness.

Am I loved by God?

Yes! God cherishes you and wants you to be close to Him. He adopted you, making you His beloved child.

Is it really possible for me to change?

Yes! You are being made new. This both *happened* to you and *is happening* to you. This means that you are changed because of what Christ has done, and you are continuing to change as you grow in Christ (it's a bit of a paradox). You can live in an ongoing process of growth by working with the Holy Spirit to become more like Christ, who loves you and gave Himself up for you.

These three life-changing events are what we mean by God's truth, the good news of Christ's finished work on our behalf—"the gospel."

Receiving God's truth and learning about the Enneagram will give you a deeper and richer understanding of *who you are* and *Whose you are*.

When we know *who we are*, we understand our heart's motives and needs, and can see God reaching out to meet our needs and giving us grace for our sins through Christ.

And when we know *Whose we are*, we understand that because of Christ's sacrifice on our behalf, we're God's cherished children. He comforts, sustains, and delights in us. Because of God's character, His love never changes; it doesn't depend on us "getting better" or "doing better" since it hinges solely on what Christ has already done for us. He loves us and desires for us to be in a relationship with Him. We become more like Him by surrendering to Him and depending on the Holy Spirit to transform us.

Which leads us back to looking at who we are. Bringing our faith and the Enneagram together helps us hear God's truths in our mother tongue (kind of like our personality Type's unique language), which enables us to understand God's truth more deeply and will lead to transformation.

Going Deeper

What things have you longed to change about yourself?

_____

_____

_____

_____

_____

_____

_____

_____

_____

How have you attempted to rescue yourself in the past or bring about change on your own? How successful were you?

_____

_____

_____

_____

What difference does knowing you belong to God make in your life?

Being Aware

We can't do anything to make God love us more or love us less since our relationship status has been taken care of solely through Christ's finished work on our behalf. And yet that doesn't mean we're not responsible for participating in our growth. That growth path will look different for different personality Types. We can use the Enneagram to help us find our unique path for transformation as we continue learning and growing. And that's what's super fun about the Enneagram! This insightful tool helps us discover *who we are* and *Whose we are*.

We are not alone on this journey of growth.

God is with us, sustaining us and providing for us. Although we're all uniquely made and no one is alike (it boggles the mind to think about it!), there are commonalities in how we think, feel, and act. The Enneagram shows us nine basic personality Types, each with its own specific patterns of thinking and ways of being: nine *valid* perspectives of the world. Getting to know each of these personality Types increases understanding, compassion, mercy, grace, and forgiveness toward ourselves and others.

Our creative God made us so diverse, yet we all reflect the essence of His character: wise, caring, radiant, creative, protective, insightful, joyful, knowledgeable, and peaceful. As we learn about ourselves and others from the Enneagram, we also learn more about God. Our strengths reflect His attributes.

So how do we begin to find our unique path for growth? By learning about the Enneagram, and by becoming aware of how our heart is doing, which isn't always easy for us. It takes a great deal of time and intentional focus. We start by observing our inner world from a *nonjudgmental* stance. (I don't know how to emphasize this enough!)

Then we can begin to recognize patterns, pause while we are in the present circumstance, and ask ourselves good, clarifying questions about *why* we are thinking, feeling, or behaving in particular ways. We can begin to identify those frustrating patterns we repeat over and over again (the ones we haven't been able to figure out how to stop) and start to think about why we keep doing them.

As I've said before, the Enneagram can act like a rumble strip on a highway, warning you when you're heading off your best path. It lets you know that if you continue in the same direction, drowsy or distracted, you might hurt yourself and others. Alerts about impending danger allow you to course correct, avoid heartache, and experience greater freedom. You will create new patterns of behavior, including a new way of turning to God, when you start to notice the rumble strips in your life.

When you're sensing a rumble strip warning, focus on the acronym AWARE:

- *Awaken*: Notice how you are reacting in your behavior, feelings, thoughts, and body sensations.
- *Welcome*: Be open to what you might learn and observe without condemnation and shame.
- *Ask*: Ask God to help clarify what is happening internally.
- *Receive*: Receive any insight and affirm your true identity as God's beloved child.
- *Enjoy*: Enjoy your new freedom from old self-defeating patterns of living.

Going Deeper

As you look back on your life, when would you have liked a rumble strip to warn you of danger?

_____

_____

_____

_____

_____

_____

In general, what causes you to veer off course and land in a common pitfall (for example, when you're worried)?

_____

_____

_____

_____

_____

_____

_____

SHARING WITH OTHERS HOW BEST TO LOVE ME

Give me freedom and space
to be my independent self.

Accept all of me just as I am.

I dislike being limited, bored,
restricted, or told what to do.

Enjoy life by being enthusiastic
and positive with me.

Listen to and enjoy my fun
stories and amazing ideas.

Laugh, have fun, and experience
the abundance of life with me.

Core Motivations

We'll begin discussing the fundamentals of the Enneagram by looking at our motivations. Your Core Motivations are the driving force behind your thoughts, feelings, and actions. The internal motivations specific to your Type help explain why you do what you do. (This is why it's impossible to discern someone else's Type. We don't know what motivates them to think, feel, and behave in particular ways. It's their Core Motivations, not their actions, that determine their Type.)

These Core Motivations consist of:

- *Core Fear*: what you're always avoiding and trying to prevent from happening
- *Core Desire*: what you're always striving for, believing it will completely fulfill you
- *Core Weakness*: the issue you're always wrestling with, which will remain a struggle until you're in heaven and is a reminder you need God's help on a daily basis
- *Core Longing*: the message your heart longs to hear

The Enneagram, like a nonjudgmental friend, names and addresses these dynamics of your heart. When you use the Enneagram from a faith-centered approach, you can see how Christ's finished work on your behalf has already satisfied your Core Longing and resolved your Core Fear, Core Desire, and Core Weakness. It's a process to learn how to live in that reality.

When we stray from the truth that we are God's beloved children, it's harder to look inside. After all,

Scripture tells us that "the heart is deceitful . . . and desperately sick" (Jeremiah 17:9). When we forget God's unconditional love for us, we respond to our weaknesses and vulnerabilities with shame or contempt, leaving us feeling worse.

When we only focus on obeying externally, we attempt to look good on the outside but never deal with the source of all our struggles on the inside.

However, when we allow ourselves to rest in the truth that Christ took care of everything for us, we can look at our inner world without fear or condemnation. Real transformation begins when we own our shortcomings.

Here are the Core Motivations of a Type 7:

- *Core Fear*: being deprived, trapped in emotional pain, limited or bored, or missing out on something fun
- *Core Desire*: being happy, fully satisfied, and content
- *Core Weakness*: being gluttonous; feeling a great emptiness inside; having an

insatiable desire to "fill yourself up" with experiences and stimulation in hopes of feeling completely satisfied and content
- *Core Longing*: "You will be taken care of."

The Enneagram exposes the condition of our heart, and it will tear down any facade we try to hide behind. Since we are God's saved children, we don't have to be afraid of judgment. We can be vulnerable because we know God has taken care of us perfectly through Christ—He has forgiven us and set us free from fear, condemnation, and shame. His presence is a safe place where we can be completely honest about where we are. With this freedom, allow the Enneagram to be a flashlight to your heart's condition. Let it reveal how you are doing at any given moment so you can remain on the best path for your personality Type.

Going Deeper

How challenging is it for you to look at the condition of your heart?

_____

_____

_____

_____

_____

_____

_____

What response do you typically have when you recognize your struggles?

_____

_____

_____

_____

_____

_____

_____

How would you like to respond when the struggles inside you are exposed?

_____

_____

_____

_____

_____

_____

_____

_____

_____

_____

_____

_____

_____

_____

_____

_____

_____

Core Fear

Understanding your Core Fear is the first step in identifying your motivations. Your personality believes it's vital to your well-being that you con-stantly spend time and energy avoiding this thing you fear. It is the lens through which you see the world, the "reality" you believe. You assume others do, or should, see the world through this lens, and you may become confused and dismayed when they don't.

Your Core Fear as a Type 7 is being deprived, trapped in emotional pain, limited or bored, or missing out on something fun.

You don't want to be around negative people

or feel inferior. You don't want to experience rest-lessness or be forced to face your fear, grief, or suffering.

Even though you fear being deprived and lim-ited, here's what is true: God will fill and satisfy you. He provides you with a never-ending resource that answers your longing in Jesus Christ.

Acknowledging, savoring, and being grateful for what you already have is key in seeing how you are not limited. God has pursued you with His love and offers you greater joy and freedom than anything on earth can bring. He does not withhold good things from His cherished children; He delights in providing for them.

When your Core Fears get activated, use them as a rumble strip to alert you. Then pause, become AWARE, and reorient yourself with what is true so your heart can rest in His provision.

MY CORE FEARS

TYPE 7
THE ENTERTAINING OPTIMIST

Being deprived, trapped in emotional pain, limited or bored, missing out on something fun

Going Deeper

What comes to mind when you think about your Core Fear?

_____

_____

_____

_____

_____

_____

_____

_____

_____

_____

Do any particular words in the Type 7 Core Fear description ring true for you?

_____

_____

_____

_____

What strategies have you used in the past to protect yourself from your fears?

Core Desire

Understanding your Core Desire is the next step in identifying your motivations. Your Core Desire is what you're always striving for, believing it will ultimately fulfill you.

While your personality Type is running away from your Core Fear, it's also running toward your Core Desire. You believe that once you have this Core Desire met, all of life will be okay and you will feel fully satisfied and content. This longing to experience your Core Desire constantly propels you to focus your efforts on pursuing and obtaining it.

As a Type 7, you desire to be happy, satisfied,

and content. You long to experience all the fullness and possibilities that life has to offer.

God knows your Core Desire, and He freely gives it to you. You have all the spiritual blessings of Christ—He did not hold back! You are not left empty. He restores you with His abundant resources that bring deep joy and satisfaction. When your heart is not content, and you long for more in life, boldly ask Him to give you satisfaction and gratitude that transcend your desire for earthly things.

Not everyone has the same Core Desire as you. Take time to recognize that others are just as passionate in obtaining their Core Desire as you are in gaining yours. This awareness will help you navigate relationship dynamics, enabling you to offer more empathy, compassion, and grace. Use the Enneagram to know yourself better so you can better communicate with others about what is happening inside your heart. Then be curious about others, and ask them to reveal to you their desires so you can get to know them on a deeper level.

MY CORE DESIRES

TYPE 7
THE ENTERTAINING OPTIMIST

Being happy, fully satisfied, and content

Going Deeper

As you look back over your life, what aspects of the Type 7 Core Desire have you been chasing?

_____

_____

_____

_____

_____

_____

_____

_____

_____

Describe ways you have attempted to pursue these specific desires.

_____

_____

_____

_____

_____

_____

_____

_____

_____

_____

_____

What would it feel like to trust in the fact that God has already met your Core Desire?

_____

_____

_____

_____

_____

_____

_____

_____

_____

_____

_____

Core Weakness

Deep inside, you struggle with a Core Weakness, which is your Achilles' heel. This one issue repeatedly causes you to stumble in life. At times you might find some relief. But as hard as you try to improve on your own, your struggle in this area continually resurfaces.

God's encouraging words to you are that when you are weak, He is strong. This brings hope that you are not destined to be utterly stuck in your weakness. As you grow closer to God and depend on Him, He will lessen the constraint your Core Weakness has over you and help you move out of your rut.

As a Type 7, your Core Weakness is *gluttony*. You feel a deep emptiness inside and have an insatiable desire to "fill yourself up" with experiences and stimulation in hopes of feeling completely satisfied and content.

The emptiness Type 7s feel is like having a large bucket inside you with holes in the bottom. You feel desperate to fill it up with exciting experiences, but the harder you try, the more you realize it isn't working. This creates panic and lots of planning and effort to rid yourself of this emptiness.

Excitement, adventures, and fun become like cotton candy. They look so good and promising but quickly disappear and cannot satisfy.

You will find satisfaction and contentment only when you turn to God, who is constantly providing for you. He is always there to meet your needs and delights in doing this for you. Ask Him to care for you and help your heart savor His everlasting love. God in His goodness answers this weakness through Christ, who is the Spring of Living Water and continually provides all you need and more. Only in coming to

Him will you become fully content. Be fully present in each moment, see what blessings are right before you, and experience deep gratitude for them.

When you see your Core Weakness surfacing, think of it as a rumble strip, alerting you that you can easily veer off course into your common pitfalls of being scattered, hyperactive, and overly reframing everything into a positive instead of dealing with the reality at hand. Use this awareness to "recalculate" your inner world so you can get back to your healthiest path.

Going Deeper

What comes to mind as you think about your Core Weakness?

_____

_____

_____

_____

_____

In what ways have you wrestled with gluttony (an insatiable need to experience stimulation and excitement) throughout your life?

_____

_____

_____

_____

_____

_____

_____

What specific things are you facing now that your Core Weakness impacts?

_____

_____

_____

_____

_____

_____

_____

TYPE 7
THE ENTERTAINING
OPTIMIST

Gluttony — feeling a great emptiness inside and having an insatiable desire to "fill yourself up" with experiences and stimulation in hopes of feeling completely satisfied and content

Core Longing

Your Core Longing is the message your heart is always yearning to receive, what you've craved since you were a child. Throughout life, you've been striving to hear this message from your family members, friends, teachers, coaches, and bosses. No matter how much you've tried to get others to communicate this message to you, you've never felt it was delivered to the degree your heart needed it.

As a Type 7, your Core Longing is to hear, "You will be taken care of."

You have believed that if you could be playful, versatile, and independent enough, then others would communicate this message to you, whether in verbal or nonverbal ways. However, even those who have tried their best to do this for you are unable to satisfy this longing that runs so deep inside you.

Why? Because people *cannot* give you all you need. Only God can. When you're trying to receive this message apart from God, you will always thirst for more. But when you listen to Him and see that He's drawing you to Himself, then you will find fulfillment and freedom.

How does God meet your Core Longing?

1. **He brings you satisfaction and contentment.**

   Christ is your stream of living water that never runs dry and is always satisfying. As His beloved child, you can enjoy as much living water as you need.

2. **He takes care of your needs.**

   Christ knew that neither others nor you could take care of all your needs, so He came to provide for all your core needs in His saving work on your behalf.

When you feel trapped or missing out, use the Enneagram as the rumble strip to alert you of what is true: that you have all your heart's needs and desires in God. Allow it to point out how you are believing false messages so you can live with more gratitude and deep joy for all of life.

Going Deeper

How have you seen your Core Longing at work in your life?

_____

_____

_____

_____

What did that look like when you were a child?

_____

_____

_____

_____

How does it appear in your life as an adult?

_____

_____

_____

_____

_____

_____

_____

_____

Describe how you feel and what you think when
you read that God answers your longing.

_____

_____

_____

_____

_____

_____

_____

_____

_____

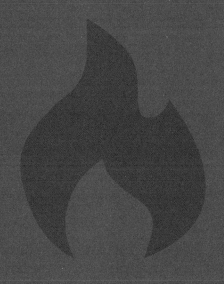

MY CORE LONGING | **TYPE 7**
THE ENTERTAINING
OPTIMIST

The message my heart always longs to hear.

"You will be taken care of."

Directional Signals of the Enneagram

Just as a GPS gives directional signals such as "Approaching right turn" or "Proceed to the high-lighted route," the Enneagram guides us in which way to go. But we still need to pay attention to where we're heading and reroute our course when necessary.

The Enneagram provides directions in a couple of ways: (1) by pointing out how aligned with God's truth we are, and (2) by showing us what other Types we are connected to and how we might take on those Types' characteristics in different life situations. We do not *become* the Types we are

YOUR INTERNAL GPS

It reveals **why** you think, feel, and behave in particular ways, so you can steer your internal life in the best direction for your personality Type.

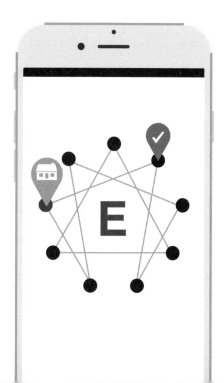

connected to; we remain our Main Type (with its Core Fear, Desire, Weakness, and Longing) as we access the other Types' attributes.

The directional signals of the Enneagram make us aware of which way our heart is heading and where we might end up. Whether it's a good or bad direction depends on various factors—it can change day by day as we take on positive or negative qualities of other Types.

When headed in the wrong direction, the steps to turning around and getting back on track are simply owning our mistakes, turning from them, asking for forgiveness from God and others, and asking God to restore us to the best path.

The directional signals we'll discuss in the following entries are: the Levels of Alignment with God's Truth, the Wings, the Triads, and the Enneagram Paths. Hang in there! I'll guide you through these signals, which will help you discover who you are and Whose you are and show you the healthiest path for your personality Type.

Type 7   HOW I TYPICALLY COMMUNICATE

When I am doing well, I speak in a fun, lively, light-hearted, upbeat, optimistic, and joyful way. I also take the time to listen to others without taking over.

When I am not doing well, I can be hyper, scattered, keep attention on myself by telling long and grand stories, reframe, and avoid anything pessimistic or too deep.

Levels of Alignment with God's Truth

The first set of directional signals we'll discuss are the Levels of Alignment with God's truth. The inspiration for these levels comes from the apostle Paul, who wrote in Galatians 2:14 that some of the early Christian leaders' conduct was not in step (aligned) with God's truth. To grow in our particular personality Type, we must be in step with God's truth and design for us.

We all move fluidly through the Levels of Alignment from day to day. The level at which we find ourselves at any given moment depends on our heart's condition and how we're navigating through life.

When we are resting, believing, and trusting in who we are in Christ, we are living as His beloved (healthy and aligned with God's truth). We are no longer using our personality strategies to meet our needs and desires. Instead, we are coming to our God, who we know loves us and will provide for us.

When our heart and mind begin to wander from that truth, we start to believe that we must take some control and live in our own strength, even though He is good and sovereign (average/auto-pilot level).

Then there are times when we completely forget that we are His beloved children. In this state of mind, we think we're all alone, that we're orphans who have to handle all of life on our own (unhealthy level).

But no matter where we are on the Levels of Alignment, we are always His cherished children. Christ's life, death, and resurrection accomplished everything required for us to be His. Therefore, no matter what state our heart is in, we can *rejoice* in His work in our lives, *repent* if we need to, and fully *rest* in who we are in Him.

As you can imagine, a group of people with the same personality Type (same Core Fear, Desire, Weakness, and Longing) can look vastly different from each other due to varying alignments with God's truth.

In the readings that follow, we will consider how you as a Type 7 function at the three Levels of Alignment.

Going Deeper

At what Level of Alignment do you think your heart is at the moment?

_____

_____

_____

_____

_____

_____

_____

_____

_____

In what season of life have you thrived the most, not feeling limited by your fears and weaknesses?

_____

_____

_____

_____

_____

_____

_____

_____

_____

_____

What do you think contributed to that growth?

_____

_____

_____

_____

_____

_____

_____

_____

_____

_____

When You Are Aligned

When the condition of your heart is healthy, you align with God's truth that you are fully taken care of by Christ.

As a Type 7 at this level, you know the joy and satisfaction you long for cannot come from the exciting experiences and constant stimulation you are tempted to place your hope in. It only comes from being in the presence of God, who fills you up with real, radiant joy. You know that being God's beloved child means you have everything you need to experience the lasting satisfaction and happiness your heart craves. You delight in simple wonders and savor things you already have.

When you are resting in this deeply gratifying place, you are able to address the difficult realities of life and deal with the sadness, disappointment, and sorrow that come with living on earth. You know that the story ends in triumph, with Christ conquering life and death. You are still playful and fun, but also principled, practical, and grounded.

Going Deeper

When are you at your best and most trusting of God?

_____

_____

_____

_____

_____

_____

_____

What differences do you notice in your thinking
and in your life when you're in that state?

_____

_____

_____

_____

_____

_____

_____

What helps you stay in alignment with God's plan
for your personality Type?

_____

_____

_____

_____

_____

_____

_____

_____

Write about a time when you've experienced true satisfaction, the ability to be grounded in the present, or any other indicators of healthy alignment.

_____

_____

_____

_____

_____

_____

_____

_____

_____

_____

_____

_____

_____

_____

_____

_____

_____

When You Are Misaligned

Even though we know God is good and in control, there are times when our hearts and minds wander away from the truth that God loves us and has fully provided for us in the finished work of Christ on our behalf. In this average or autopilot level of health, we start to believe that we must take some control and live in our own strength.

As a Type 7 at this level, you avoid any pain, sadness, or disappointment. You think you have to create new and exciting experiences to avoid feeling any discomfort.

You are a master at reframing anything negative to escape pain. You convince yourself and others

MY HIDDEN STRUGGLE
TYPE 7

The belief that I must appear
upbeat, spontaneous, and fun,
and that I must conceal the darker
emotions, anxiety, loneliness, and
frustration that bring me down

A private battle with self-doubt and
negative feelings, and the fear that I'll
always feel a deep emptiness inside

An unending desire for stimulation
or any experience that will bring me
entertainment, satisfaction, and pleasure

that there is a silver lining when something sad, upsetting, or bad happens. This strategy keeps you from living in the present reality and dealing with the situation at hand.

You might find it difficult to focus on projects, commit to relationships, and finish tasks. When others address these struggles, you tend to escape into more exciting and fun experiences to avoid feeling trapped in emotional pain or negativity. This, of course, only feeds the issue, which causes it to intensify.

Going Deeper

What aspects of your behavior and life indicate that you are becoming misaligned?

_____

_____

_____

_____

_____

In what ways do you attempt to live in your own strength, not in your identity as a person God loves?

_____

_____

_____

_____

_____

_____

_____

_____

What can you do when you begin to catch yourself in misalignment?

_____

_____

_____

_____

_____

_____

_____

When You Are Out of Alignment Entirely

When we completely forget that our status never changes, and we are still His beloved based on what Christ did for us, we think and believe we're all alone, like an orphan.

Your entire focus at this level is avoiding anything that causes you pain or boredom. You cannot tolerate restrictions or limitations placed on you, so you find ways to escape them to find pleasure. You might take more risks, become reckless, or develop an addiction.

You also feel that others are inhibiting you from a life of joy and happiness, failing to see that it is your insatiable appetite that cannot be quenched with earthly pleasures.

When you recognize that all your efforts to bring satisfaction do not work and that only God can give you deep, lasting joy, you will begin to get healthier. You will be able to rest in the presence of a God who loves you immensely and to slow down and savor the deep contentment that comes from being close with Him.

Going Deeper

In what seasons of life have you been most out of alignment with God's truth?

_____

_____

_____

_____

_____

_____

What does this level look like for you (specific behaviors, beliefs, etc.)?

_____

_____

_____

_____

_____

_____

_____

Who in your life can best support and encourage you when you're struggling and guide you back to health?

_____

_____

_____

_____

_____

_____

The Wings

The next set of directional signals we'll discuss are the Wings, which are the two numbers *directly* next to your Main Type's number on the Enneagram diagram. As I've said, we access the characteristics of the Type on either side of us while remaining our Main Type. So everyone's Enneagram personality is a combination of one Main Type and the two Types adjacent to it.

As a Type 7, your Wings are 6 and 8. You'll often see it written this way: 7w6 or 7w8.

Everyone uses their Wings to varying degrees and differently in different circumstances, but it's common for a person to rely more on one Wing than another.

You can think of the Wings like salt and pepper. Each Wing adds a unique "flavor" to your personality, bringing complexity to your Main Type. Just as a delicious filet mignon doesn't *become* the salt or pepper we season it with, we don't become our Wings. Our Wings influence our Main Type in varying ways, both positively and negatively depending on where we are on the Levels of Alignment. We know that too much salt or pepper can make that filet inedible, but the right balance can enhance our enjoyment of it significantly.

When we align with God's truth, we can access the healthy aspects of our Wings. When we are misaligned or out of alignment with God's truth, we will often draw from the average or unhealthy aspects of our Wings. And like under seasoning or over seasoning our perfectly cooked steaks, it can make a huge difference.

Learning how to use our Wings correctly can dramatically alter our life experiences. Applying "seasoning"—utilizing the healthy attributes of our Wings—can help us change course. As we return to believing and trusting in God, we can express our-selves more fully and be seen for who we really are.

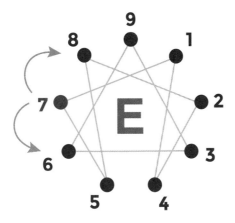

Type 7 with Wing 6 (7w6), The Entertainer: These two Types conflict with each other. Type 7 is looking for independence, freedom, and positive and stimulating experiences. Type 6 is focused on establishing supportive relationships and following trusted leaders or systems.

If you're an Entertainer, you are outgoing, desire to enjoy experiences with others, and care about what others think. You can be creative, silly, playful, and optimistic. You are more generous and tender than the Realist.

When you are struggling, the anxieties of Type 6 can cause you to lose focus and become scattered. You can seem fidgety, revved up, and impulsive, and you may seek relationships or possessions that will distract you from your anxieties.

Type 7 with Wing 8 (7w8), The Realist: This is an aggressive subtype that demands people or circumstances satisfy his or her vast desires.

If you're a Realist, you are assertive and ambitious. You have intense energy and care less about what others think than the Entertainer does. Confident and optimistic, you have an innovative spirit to overcome any obstacle or failure. With a quick mind, persistence, and tenacity, you know how to strategize to get what you want.

When you are struggling, you can be a workaholic and an adrenaline seeker. You may be direct, demanding, and aggressive with those who stand in your way, and find conflicts stimulating. You are strong-willed and fiercely independent.

Type 7 WINGS

Type 7 with 6 Wing (7w6)
"The Entertainer"
They are more loyal, endearing, responsible, outgoing, relationship-oriented, playful, childlike, and anxious.

Type 7 with 8 Wing (7w8)
"The Realist"
They are more free, passionate, adventurous, strong, seek intensity, are leaders, quick minded, and creative.

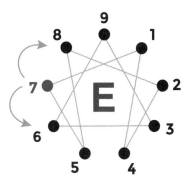

Going Deeper

Which Wing do you use more?

_____

_____

_____

_____

_____

_____

_____

_____

How have you seen this Wing enhance your Main Type?

_____

_____

_____

_____

_____

_____

_____

How does it impact your relationships, work, and everyday life?

_____

_____

_____

_____

_____

_____

_____

_____

How does the other Wing influence your Main Type?

_____

_____

_____

_____

_____

_____

_____

_____

How can you utilize it more to create balance?

_____

_____

_____

_____

_____

_____

_____

_____

_____

_____

_____

_____

_____

_____

_____

_____

_____

_____

_____

The Triads

The next set of directional signals we'll discuss are the Triads. We can group the nine personality Types in many ways, and the most common one is by groupings of three, or Triads. The three Types in each group share common assets and liabilities. For each person one Triad is more dominant (the one with your Main Type) than the other two.

Though we could name several different Triads within the Enneagram, the best known is the Center of Intelligence Triad:

- Feeling Center (Heart Triad): Types 2, 3, and 4
- Thinking Center (Head Triad): Types 5, 6, and 7
- Instinctive Center (Gut Triad): Types 8, 9, and 1

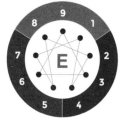

Two commonalities drive the Enneagram Types in each of these three centers: a common emotional imbalance and a common desire.

In the Head Triad, Types 5, 6, and 7 are imbalanced in their *thinking*. They all have similar assets and liabilities related to how they think and engage in life through mental analysis. They all react to their *mental struggles* with *anxiety* (or fear): Type 5s are anxious about not knowing enough to go out into the world and do. Type 6s are anxious about all the negative possibilities that could happen in any given situation. Type 7s are anxious about being forced to focus on their inner world, getting trapped in emotional pain, or feeling deprived.

Those in the Head Triad focus on a desire for *security*. Type 5s seek security through knowledge and understanding. Type 6s seek security in identifying all possible scenarios, planning for all contingencies, and having a support system in place. Type 7s seek security by avoiding their inner world of anxiety and experiencing fun, stimulation, and excitement from the external world.

When you are healthy as a Type 7, you do many things well because of your quick and creative mind.

However, when you start to struggle, you can overextend yourself with more activities than you can handle. You fear seeing and dealing with your pain and anxiety, so you escape into a world of fun experiences and stimulation, keeping your focus on exciting options and future plans.

Your mind can become restless and move from one activity to another without completing them.

ENNEAGRAM TYPE 7

At Their Best	At Their Worst
Fun-Loving	Self-Focused
Spontaneous	Impulsive
Imaginative	Escapist
Productive	Rebellious
Enthusiastic	Distracted
Quick	Superficial
Confident	Manic
Charming	Self-Destructive
Curious	Restless

You enjoy being in constant forward motion and have trouble being still, quiet, or alone for any length of time because that is when your anxieties surface. This makes you feel trapped and desperate to escape.

Going Deeper

What stands out to you about being in the Thinking Triad and your tendency to be anxious about being trapped in emotional pain?

_____

_____

_____

_____

_____

_____

_____

_____

_____

_____

How attuned are you to your feeling and gut instincts in comparison to thinking?

_____

_____

_____

_____

_____

_____

_____

In what ways do you wrestle with anxiety and a constant desire for more?

_____

_____

_____

_____

_____

_____

_____

_____

How do you respond to these struggles? Do your actions bring the satisfaction and fulfillment you want?

_____

_____

_____

_____

_____

_____

_____

Where do your strengths of being playful, versatile, and creative shine the most?

_____

_____

_____

_____

_____

_____

Childhood Message

Before we discuss the last set of directional signals (the Enneagram Paths), we need to understand what the Enneagram calls a Childhood Message.

From birth, everyone has a unique perspective on life, our personality Type's perspective. We all tend toward particular assumptions or concerns, and these develop into a Childhood Message. Our parents, teachers, and authority figures may have directly communicated this message to us, but most of the time, we interpreted what they said or did through the lens of our personality Type to fit this belief.

Sometimes we can see a direct correlation

between our Childhood Message and a childhood event; other times we can't. Somewhere, somehow, we picked up a message that rang true for us because of our personality Type's hardwiring. This false interpretation of our circumstances was and still is painful to us, profoundly impacting us as children and as adults.

Gaining insight into how our personality Type interpreted events and relationships in childhood will help us identify how that interpretation is impacting us today. Believing our Childhood Message causes our personality to reinforce its strategies to protect us from our Core Fear - apart from God's truth. Once we understand the message is hardwired into our thinking, we can experience God's healing truth and live more freely.

What's more, when we know the Childhood Message of others, we can begin to understand why they do what they do and how we can communicate with them more effectively.

As a Type 7, your Childhood Message is: "It is not okay to depend on anyone for anything."

The message your heart longed to hear as a child is your Core Longing: "You will be taken care of."

•   •   •

Type 7 children felt emotionally disconnected from their nurturing parents and believed they did not receive enough care (mainly fun and exciting experiences). The message they thought they were hearing (directly or indirectly) from authority figures was, "You are on your own. No one else is going to meet your needs to the extent you ask for."

Therefore, at an early age, they determined that they needed to nurture and care for themselves without relying on others. They took it upon themselves to find contentment and satisfaction, creating a world full of happy thoughts and exciting adventures. Then they used those distractions to flood out their painful thoughts and feelings.

Type 7s' minds are magical wonderlands with endless amazing experiences. The problem is that Type 7s are never fully satisfied. The more they try to fill themselves up on their own, the emptier they feel. They are constantly trying to find new and exciting experiences they hope will fill their inner void.

Knowing your personality Type's Childhood Message will help you break free from childhood perceptions and reinterpret pieces of your story from a better vantage point. As you explore this, be gracious to yourself and your past. Be sensitive, nonjudgmental, caring, and kind to yourself. And remember, only God can fully redeem your past. He can free you from chains that bind, heal wounds that linger, and restore you to freedom.

Going Deeper

To what degree do you relate to the Type 7 Childhood Message?

_____

_____

_____

_____

What stories come to mind when you hear it?

_____

_____

_____

_____

_____

_____

_____

_____

What circumstances in the present have repeated this message from the past?

_____

_____

_____

_____

_____

_____

_____

What advice would you give to your childhood self
in light of this message?

Enneagram Paths

The final directional signals we'll discuss are the Enneagram Paths, which the inner lines and arrows in the Enneagram diagram display. The lines and arrows going out from our Main Type point to our Connecting Types. As a Type 7, you connect to Types 1 and 5.

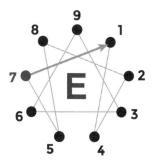
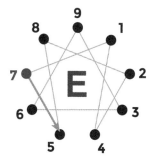

Remember, we can access both positive and negative characteristics of a Type we are connected to. The kind we access depends on whether we are aligned, misaligned, or out-of-alignment with God's truth.

Here is an overview of the four Enneagram Paths, which we'll discuss further in the following readings:

- *Stress Path*: When we're under stress, we tend to take on some of the misaligned or out-of-alignment characteristics of our Stress Path Type. For Type 7, these are the negative aspects of Type 1.
- *Blind Spot Path*: When we're around those we're most familiar with (mainly family), we display the misaligned characteristics of our Blind Spot Path Type. We typically do not see these characteristics in ourselves easily. For Type 7, these are the negative aspects of Type 5.
- *Growth Path*: When we believe and trust that

God loves us and that all He has is ours in Christ, we begin to move in a healthier direction, accessing the aligned characteristics of our Connecting Type. For Type 7, these are the positive aspects of Type 5.

- *Converging Path*: After making progress on the Growth path, we can reach the most aligned point of our Type, which is where three healthy Types come together. Here we access the healthiest qualities of our Main Type, our Growth Path's Type, and our Stress Path's Type.

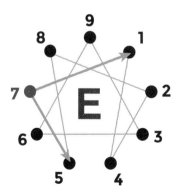

Going Deeper

In what direction is your heart currently heading?

_____

_____

_____

_____

_____

_____

_____

_____

What concerns are you wrestling with?

_____

_____

_____

_____

_____

_____

_____

_____

What growth have you experienced recently?

_____

_____

_____

_____

_____

_____

_____

_____

_____

When you look at the four paths, what path have you been traveling recently? Why?

_____

_____

_____

_____

_____

_____

_____

_____

Stress Path

Under stress, you tend to move in the direction of the arrow below, taking on some of the misaligned characteristics of Type 1. Learning to identify these behavior patterns can serve as a rumble strip warning that you're veering off course. Then you can

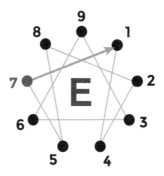

stop, pray for God's help, and move in a healthier direction for your personality.

As a Type 7 moving toward the average or unhealthy Type 1, you may:

- impose restrictions and limitations on yourself to be more productive.
- become more irritable and critical of yourself.
- notice and point out imperfections in yourself, others, and the world.
- become perfectionistic and judgmental, wanting others to live up to higher ideals.
- get upset with others who are preventing you from experiencing fun.
- micromanage those you feel are not being responsible.

Going Deeper

Describe a stressful time when you took on some of these tendencies.

_____

_____

_____

_____

_____

_____

_____

What was the situation, and why were you triggered to respond this way?

_____

_____

_____

_____

_____

_____

_____

_____

What things in your life cause the most stress for you?

TYPE 7 UNDER STRESS

When under stress, **Type 7** will start to exhibit some of the average to unhealthy characteristics of **Type 1**.

Becoming a perfectionist and critical

Becoming cynical and hypercritical to change people

Blaming others for preventing fun

Blind Spot Path

When you're around people you're most familiar with—family members or close friends—you express yourself more freely. You show them parts of yourself you don't show anyone else, for better or worse. When you're uninhibited and not at your best, you display the negative qualities of your personality. On this Blind Spot Path, you access the misaligned attributes of your Connecting Type, which is Type 5.

You may be unaware that you're behaving differently with your family members or close friends than you are with other people. Be sure to take note of this path when you're trying to understand yourself and your reactions, because it may surprise you. Working on these negative aspects can improve the relationship dynamics with those you're closest to.

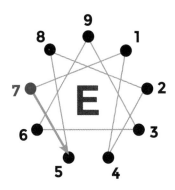

As a Type 7 moving toward the average or unhealthy Type 5, you may:

- withdraw and seek seclusion to recharge.
- tire of always being positive.
- conserve your energy by becoming less excitable and more of an observer.
- have fewer positive feelings about your life situation.

- experience dark, cynical, and pessimistic viewpoints.
- struggle to trust people and prefer not to be around them.

Going Deeper

How do you respond when you feel overwhelmed in the presence of people you feel secure with versus those you're less comfortable with?

_____

_____

_____

_____

_____

_____

_____

_____

_____

_____

Which of the average or unhealthy tendencies do you resonate with the most?

_____

_____

_____

_____

_____

_____

_____

_____

Describe a situation where you reacted in the ways described above.

_____

_____

_____

_____

_____

_____

_____

_____

Growth Path

When you believe and trust that God loves you, and all He has is yours, you begin to relax and let go of your personality's constraints and lies. You draw nearer to Him and move in a direction that aligns you with His truth. You feel safe, secure, and loved.

Feeling more joy, peace, and liberation, you stretch yourself toward healthier attributes, even though it is hard. As you grow in faith and depend solely on Him, God blesses you with real and lasting transformation, shaping you into who He made you to be.

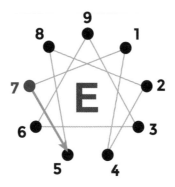

As a Type 7 moving toward the healthy side of Type 5, you can:

- focus on your inner world and learn to relax.
- allow your quick mind to rest instead of being hyperactive, finding more clarity and insight.
- accomplish tasks in line with your passions by becoming more organized and structured.
- become grounded, focused, and more profound.
- place more value on wisdom and discipline.
- become more accepting of all of life—good and bad, happy and sad.

Going Deeper

When you are growing, what changes about your heart and your typical responses?

_____

_____

_____

_____

_____

_____

Which of these growth attributes would you love to experience more in your life?

_____

_____

_____

_____

_____

_____

_____

What helps to support your growth and flourishing?

_____

_____

_____

_____

_____

_____

_____

_____

_____

How can you incorporate those things into your
life more?

_____

_____

_____

_____

_____

_____

_____

_____

TYPE 7 DIRECTION OF **GROWTH**

When moving in the direction of growth, **Type 7** will start to exhibit some of the healthier characteristics of **Type 5**.

Learning how to deal with their uncomfortable feelings and relax in the present moment

Having a quieter mind enables them to focus and draw out more creativity and depth

Experiencing each moment as fascinating and profound

Converging Path

You are your best self on the Converging Path, where three Types come together. Here you access the healthiest qualities of your Main Type, your Growth Path's Type, and your Stress Path's Type. When you live in the fullness of who you really are in Christ, you are freed from the bonds of your personality.

This path of personal transformation can be difficult to reach and maintain. When you first learn about the Converging Path, you may feel it's too hard to travel. But God wants to provide this path for you. Trust Him, follow Him, and ask Him to be with you as you move forward.

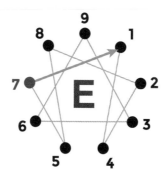

As a Type 7 moving toward the healthy side of Type 1, you may:

- learn to accept life as it is and live for a higher purpose.
- focus on your top priority and complete it on time without avoiding it.
- accomplish tasks well and with accuracy.
- slow down and take your time to make sure things are done right.
- take ownership of your responsibilities even if they are not fun.

Going Deeper

Can you recall a time when you experienced the freedom and joy of the Converging Path?

_____

_____

_____

_____

_____

_____

What was it like when you accessed the healthiest aspects of your Main Type, Growth Path's Type, and Stress Path's Type?

_____

_____

_____

_____

_____

_____

_____

What would help you move toward your Converging
Path more often?

_____

_____

_____

_____

_____

_____

_____

_____

_____

_____

_____

_____

_____

_____

_____

_____

_____

_____

Spiritual Renewal

TYPE 7
THE ENTERTAINING OPTIMIST

GOING DEEPER
Grab a journal and make a list of everything you're thankful for. Reflect on all the ways God has blessed your life, the gifts you've been given, and everything that brings you joy in the present moment. Ask God to remind you that only He brings true contentment and satisfaction.

Moving Toward Your Best Self

The journey of exploring your heart is not an easy one, but it's an exciting one.

God has a unique message for each Type. The message He tells you as a Type 7 is: "You can be perfectly satisfied and content because I fulfill your needs."

You have tried to fill yourself with all kinds of enjoyable experiences, but they have left you empty and needing more.

Only Christ can provide the care and tenderness your heart craves. The love and life He gives is rich and joyful, and penetrates the emptiness you feel inside. He will always satisfy your curiosity and need for stimulation because He is never dull or boring.

God knows that you long to experience all of life fully (happiness, sadness, joy, disappointment), and He provides a calm and safe place for you to do that. You will find a purer joy when you allow yourself to feel all your emotions and open up to God, who will always understand and care for you.

Each Type has a signature Virtue, which you exhibit when you are at your best, and Type 7's Virtue is *sobriety*.

At your best, you allow your mind to slow down, be present in life, and savor the goodness all around you. This enables you to experience happiness, overflowing gratitude, and a richer depth to your life.

With your hungry heart satisfied by God's love for you, you feel a lasting fullness, no longer desperate to be filled up. You can focus on others instead of your cravings and desires, and let others express themselves without reframing any negativity or sadness into something positive. You can sit in uncomfortable spaces, knowing that God will fully take care of you and the situation at hand.

Using the Enneagram from a biblical perspective can empower you to see yourself with astonishing clarity so you can break free from self-condemnation, fear, and shame by experiencing unconditional love, forgiveness, and freedom. In Him, you are whole. And with Him by your side, you can grow stronger and healthier every day.

Now that you know how to use this internal GPS and its navigational signals, start using it every day. Tune in to how your heart is doing. Avoid your common pitfalls by staying alert to your rumble strips. As you learn new awareness and actions, you will move forward on the path that is healthiest for your personality Type and experience the gift of tremendous personal growth.

Going Deeper

What do you notice about yourself when you're at your best?

_____

_____

_____

_____

_____

_____

_____

What would the world be like without the involvement of healthy Type 7s?

_____

_____

_____

_____

_____

_____

_____

Type 7 VIRTUE

Sobriety is your virtue.

This allows you to feel sober and awake and fully present in all experiences as if every moment were completely new and unique.

What are some practical ways you can offer your virtue to others today?

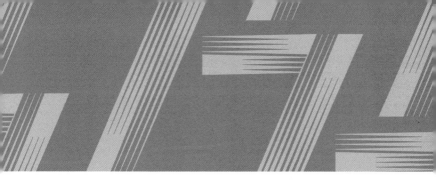

Afterword

God's plan to restore the world involves all of us, which is why He made us so vastly different from each other in ways that reflect who He is.

That is why I'm so thrilled you picked up this book and have done the hard, but rewarding, work of looking into your heart. When you align with God's truth, you can support the kingdom, knit people together, and be the best *you* only you can be.

Growth is *not* easy. It requires us to surrender to God, depend on Him, and walk into His calling for us. But when we let go of our control and He takes over, He will satisfy our hearts, filling them with His goodness, and His blessings will flow into our lives and others' lives.

I can attest to God's transformative work having this ripple effect—reaching and positively impacting different parts of our lives and everyone we encounter. As I became more aligned with God's truth (and make no mistake, I'm still in progress!), the changes I was making helped transform my relationships with Jeff, my family, and other people around me. More and more friends, acquaintances, and even strangers were experiencing the transformation that comes from God through the tool of the Enneagram.

I can't wait to look back a year from now, five years from now, or even a decade from now, and hear about the ripple effects *your* transformation has created for hope, wholeness, and freedom. I'm excited about the path of discovery and growth ahead of you! What is God going to do in you with this new understanding of yourself and those around you? What are the things you'll hear Him whisper in your heart that will begin to set you free?

And how will your personal transformation bring positive change to the people in your life?

This is what I hope for you: First, that you will believe and trust in your identity in Christ. In Him, you are forgiven and set free. God delights in having you as His dear child and loves you unconditionally. This reality will radically change everything in you—it is the ultimate transformation from death to life.

Second, I hope that as you discover more about your Enneagram Type, you'll recognize how your personality apart from Christ is running *away* from your Core Fear, running *toward* your Core Desire, *stumbling* over your Core Weakness, and *desperate* to have your Core Longing met. As you become aware of these traits, you can make them the rumble strip alarms that point out what's going on in your heart. Then you can ask the Holy Spirit to help you navigate your inner world and refocus your efforts toward traveling the best path for your personality Type.

Third, I hope that God will reveal to you, both

in knowledge and experience, the transformative work of the Holy Spirit. With Him you can move toward growth, using all the tools of the Enneagram (the Levels of Alignment, the Wings, the Triads, the Enneagram Paths, etc.) to bring out the very best in you, the way God designed you to be. As a result, others will be blessed, God will be glorified, and you will experience the closeness of a Savior who will always meet your every longing and need.

May the love of Christ meet you where you are and pull you closer to God and others. And may you experience the joy of knowing His love for you in a deeper and more meaningful way.

Acknowledgments

My husband: I have to start by thanking my incredible husband, Jeff, who is my biggest cheerleader and supporter. He has helped me use the Enneagram from a biblical perspective and lovingly ensured that I expanded my gifts. Without his encouragement each step of the way, I never would have ventured into this world of writing. Thank you so much, Jeff.

My kids: Nathan and Libby McCord, you are a gift and blessing to me, and an inspiration for the work I do. Thank you for affirming me, being patient with me, and always believing in me. I pray this resource will bless you back as you journey through life.

My family: To my incredible parents, Dr. Bruce and Dana Pfuetze, who have always loved me well and encouraged me to move past difficulties by relying on the Lord. To my dear brother and sister-in-law, Dr. Mark and Mollie Pfuetze, thank you for being a source of support.

My team at Your Enneagram Coach: You enable me to be the best I can be as a leader, and I'm so honored to be a part of our amazing team. Thank you for letting me serve, for showing up every day, and for helping those who want to become more like Christ by using the Enneagram from a biblical perspective. Thank you, Danielle Smith, Traci Lucky, Robert Lewis, Lindsey Castleman, Justin Barbour, and Monica Snyder.

My marketing team, Well Refined Co.: Thank you, Christy Knutson, Jane Butler, JoAnna Brown, and Madison Church.

My agent: Thank you, Bryan Norman, for helping me navigate through all the ins and outs so that this could be the very best work for our readers. Your advice was most beneficial.

ACKNOWLEDGMENTS

My publisher: To Adria Haley and the team at HarperCollins Christian, thank you for allowing me to share my passion for the Enneagram with the world in such a beautiful way through this book collection.

My writing team at StrategicBookCoach.com: Thank you, Danielle Smith, Karen Anderson, and Sharilyn Grayson for helping me create my manuscript.

My friend and advisor: Writing a book is harder than I expected and more rewarding than I could have ever imagined. None of this would have been possible without my most-cherished friend and beloved advisor, Karen Anderson. I am thankful for her heart, her passion, and her help every step of the way. You beautifully take my concepts and make them sing. Thank you!

About the Author

Beth McCord has been using the Enneagram in ministry since 2002 and is a Certified Enneagram Coach. She is the founder and lead content creator of Your Enneagram Coach and cowrote *Becoming Us: Using the Enneagram to Create a Thriving Gospel-Centered Marriage* with her husband, Jeff. Beth has been featured as an Enneagram expert in magazines and podcasts and frequently speaks at live events. She and Jeff have two grown children, Nate and Libby, and live in Franklin, Tennessee, with their blue-eyed Australian Shepherd, Sky.

Continue Your Personal Growth Journey *Just for Type 7!*

Get your Type's in-depth online coaching course that is customized with guide sheets and other helpful insights so you can continue uncovering your personal roadmap to fast-track your growth, overcome obstacles, and live a more fulfilling life with God, others, and yourself.

VISIT YOURENNEAGRAMCOACH.COM/EXPLORING-YOU

The mission of YourEneagramCoach.com is for people to see themselves with astonishing clarity so they can break free from self-condemnation, fear, and shame by knowing and experiencing unconditional love, forgiveness, and freedom in Christ.